Newmarket
in old picture postcards

by Mary S. Basham

European Library ZALTBOMMEL/THE NETHERLANDS

GB ISBN 90 288 3282 3

© 1985 European Library – Zaltbommel/The Netherlands

Fourth edition, 1998: reprint of the original edition of 1985.

INTRODUCTION

Nobody could accuse Newmarket of being a 'one horse town' for there are literally hundreds of the equine aristocrats around and about the place. Any morning sees strings of them stepping out from their stables, wending their way through the busy traffic as they make for the gallops or the beech woods beside the Bury road. A photographer's dream and one which has been captured many times over the last one hundred years, confirming Newmarket's place, not only in reality but on film, as the capital of British horseracing.

But has it always been like this? The short answer is no! Newmarket's existence began simply as that, a new market created from two parishes that lay either side of an ancient track, the Icknield Way. Its connection with the horse arose four centuries later, when James I came to hunt hare in the fields of Fordham on Wednesday 27th February 1605 and enjoyed the sport so much he decided to build a royal residence in nearby Newmarket. Here he returned frequently throughout his reign, to savour the excitement of testing the speed of horses over the springy heathland; hardly the highly organised sport we know today, but the essence of it.

A succession of monarchs have followed suit, including James own son, Charles I, who also enjoyed the sport but may well have taken less pleasant memories of the town to his early grave. For it was in the palace built by his father, that he was held under house arrest by Cromwell's men before being carted off to stand trial for treason.

There then followed a period of restraint for the town as Puritan rule clamped down, particularly in the eastern counties, the Lord Protector's birthplace. However, nothing lasts forever and come the Restoration, Charles II built himself a royal residence in Newmarket and breathed life back into the idea of racing horses against each other. He too visited the town so frequently that some referred to Newmarket as the second capital of England and although his followers may not have always appreciated the weeks away from London, they were forced to take lodgings locally and many found accommodation in the network of rows that made up the old Rookery. The life of the town bustled along at a merry pace, the Court wined and dined in the many inns and hostelries and watched cock-fighting Mains as a 'diversion', until the Great Fire of 1683 sent them scurrying back to London and in doing so, defeated the Rye House Plot.

A century later finds the Jockey Club installed in a coffee house on the High Street; royal patronage is no longer essential but often forthcoming. Rules and regulations govern the administration of the Turf and great advances in breeding come with the introduction of Arabian stock.

And so it continued, a town bound up with the Turf, while at the same time acting as a market place for the surrounding villages and as a staging post for coaches along the London to Norwich road. By the late 1800s it had its own workhouse, gasworks, hospital, fledgling electric light company and in keeping with its origin from two parishes in different counties, two sets of schools and courthouses, one in St. Mary's and the county of Suffolk, one in All Saints and the county of Cambridgeshire.

The photographs and postcards in this book reflect that bustling life from a hundred years ago until the 1930s, a time when the gentry came to stay in their elegant houses for the meetings, the Prince of Wales, later King Edward VII, had his own suite of rooms at the Jockey Club and a large proportion of employment in the area was either directly or indirectly linked to horseracing. Whether it was the golden age would be difficult to say, and it would be impossible to compare it to the present day, for so much has changed. A by-pass has moved traffic away from the old travellers route down the High Street, the market has been transferred to a new, open complex called the Rookery, but nothing like the original, and light industry aims to provide an alternative form of employment — but there is still the horse and today's Arab influence comes by way of the people who own many of them.

Acknowledgements

I would like to acknowledge all the research and dedication the town's history has received from Canon Peter May, and on a different level, from my own students over the last two years in the 'Look Back at Newmarket' class at the Adult Education Centre, Foley House. My grateful thanks go to all those who lent me postcards and photographs, and to the Suffolk Record Office and Cambridgeshire Collection for giving me permission to use some of their material. I would also like to thank Ilford Ltd., for film sponsorship and Jeremy Pembrey, Photography, who carried out all the initial printing and developing. Finally, I dedicate this book to Ian Nelson, who, despite his protests to the contrary, is a walking encyclopaedia on the town and the surrounding district.

August 1985   Mary Basham

1. In keeping with its origin of being created from two parishes in two different counties, Newmarket designated its High Street to form the boundary between St. Mary's in Suffolk and All Saints in Cambridgeshire. This picture gives you some idea of how the High Street stretched out through the heart of the town, from the clock tower at this end, to the trees at the top of The Terrace in the distance. When this photograph was taken in the late 1890s, the shop on the right with the striped blind, belonged to Hugo Waugh, who sold highclass provisions and catered in general for the gentry. Many older residents remember Miss Waugh serving behind the counter and the fact that she always wore a frilled apron. Alongside Waugh's stood Barrow's, the chemists, with the old Crown Hotel next door. Both had had their fronts built up in line with fashion and the other houses in the street.

2. A rare look at one of Newmarket's well-known inns, The Crown, with its pretty Dutch gabling and sun blinds, situated at the top end of the High Street, near Woolworth's. It was under the management of the Bloss family for many years and in the 1880s Annie Bloss was in charge. Next door is Dunning, the chemist, which used to be the premises of William Barrow, pharmacist, one of the famous Barrow family who were involved in various forms of medicine in the town. The large house adjoining The Crown, Mentmore House, belonged to George Owen Mead and George Borwick Mead, surgeons and Medical Health Officers at the Rous Memorial Hospital.

Clock Tower & Bury Road,
Newmarket

3. The prominent clock tower which stands at the eastern end of the High Street was erected by the town to commemorate Queen Victoria's Golden Jubilee of 1887. When a permanent reminder was first suggested various schemes had been proposed for clearing the old Corn Exchange site and building a new Public Hall. Nothing came of this idea and the Jubilee Committee in charge of proceedings, finally settled on a tower to hold a clock which had been donated by Mr. Charles Blanton. Over eighty designs were submitted before the Committee came to an agreement on the one we see today. The four fine lamps shown on this postcard of 1911 were very much an afterthought. When the Town Board refused to meet their cost, the Jubilee Committee paid for them out of their own pockets.

THE SEVERALS, NEWMARKET. 9502

4. A fine view of the Severals taken around 1905. The exact meaning of the word Several is not known in this instance but is probably derived from the context 'a piece of common assigned for a period to a particular occupier'. As far as the town's people are concerned, it has always been used for public events, including the celebration of Guy Fawke's night when it has long been the site of a big bonfire. It has also played its part as a venue for visiting circuses, and in 1902 saw great excitement when two elephants escaped and forced open the door of Mr. Leach's premises close by. A startled local 'Bobby' summoned the keeper, who found the marauders contentedly munching their way through a quantity of carrots they had discovered. It took a lot of persuasion to entice them back to their pens!

J&S. 7099. High Street & Jubilee Tower, Newmarket.

5. Bury end of the High Street taken from the corner of the Severals about 1904. The trees on the right stand in the garden of The Chestnuts, a large black timber-framed building with stable yard and spacious lawns, once the home of Ernest and Robert Fyson, surgeons. On the other side was a veterinary surgeon's, man and beast catered for within a few yards. Lower down on the corner of Rous Road, 'Ducker Gilbert', saddlers and harnessmaker, had his premises. Downstairs a large Georgian fireplace was kept well filled with glowing coals to draw customers for a warm and a chat while they placed their orders. Upstairs 'silkmakers' worked by candlelight and the heat from a tortoise boiler. Wages were low and the hours long, particularly in the Flat season when employees could expect to work until at least 8 o'clock at night.

6. Bury Road at the turn of the century, showing the Severals on the left and the neat avenue of recently planted trees stretching away towards the Bury St. Edmunds turn-off in the distance. Despite its importance as a main route, Bury Road was one of the worst roads in the town and the cause of several accidents. Its surface was covered with horse manure and according to the season, was either a sea of mud or deeply rutted and dusty. The Local Board of Health was constantly receiving complaints about it and other roads in the town, which they attempted to improve by buying a horse-hoe in 1883. This was not a great success and their accounts then show annual bills for granite chippings and eventually, the purchase of a steam roller in 1893.

7. A good view of the 'Chestnuts' on the right and of the Rutland Arms, previously known as The Ram, in the middle distance. Popular legend would have us believe that The Ram was named after the Lord Orford incident when the sporting gentleman is said to have driven his four-in-hand team of stags into the inn's yard when chased by the Essex Hounds. Fortunately a quick-thinking stable lad 'rammed' shut the gates and saved the team from disaster. However attractive a theory this may seem, it would appear to bear little resemblance to the truth as the inn was known as The Ram long before this story is said to have taken place. It was not unusual though for hounds to pass through the town in pursuit, and one such incident is recorded in January 1895, when Mr. Walter Greene's Staghounds chased their quarry through the High Street and out the other side.

8. An unusual photograph of the Rutland Arms courtyard taken in the 1890s and showing some charming domestic touches, like the row of service bells over the archway, the log basket waiting to be filled and a pile of mats by the back door. It is almost a scene unchanged to the modern day but the inn itself has had a long and chequered history. The original inn dated back to the 1400s when it was known as The Ram and although nothing of that remains accept the site, some parts of the present structure were built in the time of Charles II. The façade is pure Georgian though, designed by John Kent a few months after the Battle of Waterloo. Over the solid, sash, first-floor windows, the Rutland family coat of arms carries the motto 'Pour y Parvenir' – To attain – and certainly the inn has always aimed at attaining the highest standards of catering and has played host to many celebrated people.

9. A classic scene from another age, the High Street on a race day in the 1890s and judging from the angle of the shadows, probably taken around mid-day. This may well account for the fact that there are few people about as we might assume they are at lunch and the cabs and carriages are waiting for their custom. Hansom cabs were the equivalent of today's taxis and it is interesting to note that they were subject to traffic offences, just like we are, but for different reasons. At the Petty Sessions held in Newmarket in May 1904, Philip Stocker, cabman, was ordered to pay 2/6d and 7/6d costs for leaving a hansom cab unattended in the High Street. No wonder small boys were often dropped a penny to look after the horse while the cab man was engaged elsewhere.

10. An attractive range of shops on the High Street lying between the Rutland Arms and the Congregational Church. This photograph was taken in the 1890s, probably by Sherborn, Newmarket's notable photographer, whose name can clearly be seen over the first shop window. Almost a century later, several of the businesses are still trading under their original names. Next door to Sherborn's is Quants, a boot and shoe shop, and alongside, Goldings, no longer in the same place, but still on the High Street, further down. Perhaps the best known of all is Wiggs, seen here proudly displaying its own flag, a gesture much appreciated by the local people at the time, who used it as an unofficial weathervane. Part of this frontage was previously occupied by Charles II royal residence, pulled down some years earlier when it was sold off by Crown agents.

11. A grand house on a grand site, for Mr. Leopold De Rothchild's Palace Hotel was built, as the name suggests, on part of the land once occupied by Charles II's royal palace. Mr. Leopold De Rothchild's marriage to Miss Maria Perugia had taken place in London on 19th January 1881 and had been marked locally by a dinner in the Public Hall for 'two hundred of the working class'. Musical entertainment was provided by Mr. Frye and friends and the Rector of Burwell had presided. Later that year Leopold De Rothchild acquired land which fronted onto Palace Street and today a magnificant house still stands there, shut away from the normal bustle of the town. Together with Palace House Stables, which lie directly opposite, the Rothchild's house provides a tangible reminder of Newmarket's royal connections.

12. Cavalry negotiating the busy High Street during the First World War with horses, which as one onlooker remarked, 'didn't look up to much'. The trap on the left had travelled in from London Farm, Isleham, a Fenland village, and Mrs. Fuller has just alighted with an order of butter for the Wigg family. (Note, butter was then traditionally sold in long rolls). Her son Tom is holding the pony's head, while daughter Ethel sits up front. The Fuller's regularly brought produce into town to fulfill standing orders or for sale in the local market, confirming Newmarket as the natural outlet for all the surrounding villages. This is still true today and any Tuesday or Saturday will find fruit, vegetables or seeds which have been produced locally on sale from stalls on the Rookery market. The photograph was loaned by Ethel Fuller who was really christened Etheldreda after the patroness of nearby Ely Cathedral. She still lives in Isleham with her sister Ruby and remembers the time when they used to go to town by trap with great clarity.

High Street, Newmarket

13. A very early morning shot of the High Street showing a string of horses on their way to exercise. Most of the shops are not open yet and it may well be market day as wooden barrows are drawn up on either side of the road waiting for the traders. The tall building, half way down on the right-hand side, is the Carlton Hotel and can only just have been built when this photo was taken in 1905. Originally the site was occupied by The Greyhound until 1889 when it was converted into high-class flats called Victoria Mansions. As for the Carlton, it survived until 1977, complete with sauna for the jockeys, its own cinema, and Winter Gardens with a fountain fed by a spring in the basement. Boots the Chemists now stand in its place, but the people of the town still remember it with affection.

14. The Greyhound yard and stabling looking quite picturesque, with its profusion of plants and neatly swept entrance, showing the ridged section down the middle which acted, not only as a means of drainage but also to prevent horses from slipping. Throughout most of the 1800s the Greyhound 'Hotel' provided good class accommodation for travellers and race-goers and acted as a posting inn for coaches to Bury St. Edmunds and London. When it was put up for sale by its owner, Mrs. Jarvis, in January 1883, it attracted a bid of £4,600, quite a high price for the time but not enough to reach the reserve. It was eventually sold a few years later and converted into the Victoria before ultimately being demolished to re-emerge as the much loved Carlton.

15. The High Street on Market Day and judging by the way that everyone except the cat is staring at the camera, it was a novelty to have a photographer present. This was taken from outside the Congregational Church and Ashfords are sited on the other side of the road from their current position. As you can see, the stalls line either side of the road, cheek by jowl with the resident traders, and there is just about enough room to get two horse-drawn vehicles through the gap. Shop assistants were more than willing to bring your orders out to the trap for you, to spare you having to step down onto the dusty road, no bad thing on this occasion, as it looks as if the horse-hoe has not been used lately! Stalls continued to line the road on Market Day until quite recently and as the High Street formed a part of the A45 until the completion of the by-pass, shopping could be hazardous.

16. For a small town, Newmarket was quite well off for churches, with St. Mary's and All Saints occupying the most prominent places on either side of the county boundary, the Wesleyan Chapel off Mill Hill, St. Agnes, built by the Duchess of Montrose, along the Bury Road and the Congregational Church, right on the High Street. The latter's rather grand structure, complete with clocktower, weathervane and tiny lantern, stood next to Golding's, with Henry Martin's, draper and milliner, on the other side. The church's elaborate railings along the front made an ideal place to park your bike when out shopping, or even to tie a horse to when necessary! There is still a church in virtually the same place, but nothing like the one in the picture. Today it shares the site with a supermarket.

17. Among the fourteen butchers trading at the beginning of the century, was W. Harper who had his premises in Wellington Street. Like many of the others, he too had his own secret sausage recipe and valued the high reputation his home-reared meat achieved. This Christmas picture, taken before the First World War, shows the shop front putting on its own festive display. Note the heads are left on the lamb carcases and each is decorated with evergreen and paper flowers. Descendants of this firm are still in business as pork butchers and continue to make excellent sausages, as winners of the annually held Town Plate race will testify, for some of The Pork Shop's produce are regularly included in the prizes.

18. Very early postcard of the High Street taken at what is known as 'the bottom end'. On the right is the old front of the Jockey Club with the Subscription Rooms, now the Horseracing Museum, alongside. To the left, with the flower filled window boxes is the White Hart, still there but now looking slightly different. The White Hart was in fact one of the busiest inns in the town at the turn of the century. It was used, not only by those with a thirst, but by auctioneers who wanted a convenient place for property sales and by clubs and societies for wining and dining. The annual dinner for the Society for the Prosecution of Felons was held there, (now it is held on the racecourse) and so was the Volunteer Ball, a once a year get-together for what we would call, the territorial element of the Suffolk Regiment.

19. The White Hart yard taken on a quiet afternoon in the 1890s. In the background the spire of St. Mary's watches over its domain in the Suffolk half of the town and seems to keep a particular eye on the inn and its patrons. The two men lowering the cask are taking their life in their hands, as this method of handling these awkward shapes often proved disastrous. One young lad was severely crushed in much the same way and had to be rushed to Addenbrooke's Hospital in Cambridge because the local infirmary could not cope with the injuries. Standing on the right, is the afternoon coach to Ipswich waiting to be hitched up to its team, as the White Hart served as the town's main posting inn. Coaches left daily for Cambridge, Ipswich and London and every other day to Fakenham, Holt, Thetford and Great Yarmouth.

20. The Jockey Club moved to Newmarket from London in 1771 and found a home in a coffee house on the High Street. Over the years various alterations and additions were made and this view of the façade shows what it must have looked like before the Club underwent a massive reconstruction during the 1930s. Fortunately, Professor Richardson, who drew up the modern design, had a sense of history and retained the original coffee room as part of the ground floor, so that even today, members can still enjoy the rarefied atmosphere of the Georgian meeting place within the new neo-Georgian style building.

21. With no official residence in Newmarket after the old royal palace was put up for sale by Victoria in 1850, Edward VII used his prerogative as a member and stayed at the Jockey Club. There, a suite of rooms overlooking the gardens was put aside for him and a special entrance constructed at the side, to give him private access. After dinner he would often enjoy a game of cards in the Club's fine Card Room where members were once required to supply their own candles for the silver holders at the corners of each table. This in turn, gave rise to the expression 'the game's not worth the candle' when some members took their loosing badly. Touches of the King's great love of the Turf still adorn some of the rooms, including the Outer Hall where a Christmas card he once sent to Persimmon hangs in a prominent place.

22. The majority of visitors to Newmarket today make for the National Horseracing Museum which was opened by Her Majesty the Queen on 30th April 1983. It contains a wide-ranging collection of pictures, documents and objects which bring the history of the Turf alive, even for those who know virtually nothing about the sport. The whole museum is housed within the old Subscription Rooms attached to the Jockey Club and this photograph, taken in 1896, shows the well-laid out lawn and walled in grounds where members could walk undisturbed. Although the building has been modified to adjust to its new roll in life, there is still a gracious air of privilege about the place and the gardens remain immaculate.

23. Taken about 1890, this rather leisurely view of the High Street suggests very little has changed over the years, although on closer inspection there are small discrepancies which set it apart from the present day. On the extreme left, in partial view, is Hammond's Bank, a long established family firm, now Barclays. Next door, the gap was known as Bird's Alley and adjoining that, complete with temperature gauge on the wall, is the easily recognised Tindalls, a printers and stationers who have been on the same site for well over a century. Shortly after this photograph was taken, the two first floor windows on the left, were made into a decorative bay, while the ground floor frontage has been altered several times. Tindalls are locally famous for their maps and guides and still maintain an old 'Eagle' printing press alongside their more modern equipment.

24. Race Day and the High Street could get as conjested as any modern traffic jam, with carriages and carts sometimes four deep. A constant shuttle service operated until the first race, taking people out to the course from the town's many hotels and inns. The 'Specials' were met by transport from the Rutland Arms and the White Hart in an attempt to secure custom. The cart with the canopy in the photograph, is typical of the type of vehicle used by carriers, the cheap form of public transport before the coming of the omnibus. It was four-wheeled, with straight sides and bench seats where passengers sat facing each other, knee to knee. Usually the horse was so used to the route that he could find his own way home, which was just as well, as after the carrier had despatched his business, he would often kill time sampling the ale before making the return journey!

25. Boyce and Rogers occupied a prominent position in the High Street sandwiched between Eaton House and the old post office on one side and T.E. Simpson, later Gilbert's and Henry Hambling, ladies outfitter, milliner, costumier and tailor, on the other. They were saddlers and harness makers of such excellence that they could guarantee to make up any saddle between the weight of one pound complete and twenty-eight pounds. Racing colours were also a speciality and these, together with horse clothing, was exported by them all over the world. One of the things best remembered about their window display was a life-sized stuffed horse which used to peer out at customers. When it was loaned to Olympia to demonstrate early motorised horseboxes, it is said it was so convincing that the Queen Mother was seen to pat it on passing.

26. A later view of the eastern end of the High Street probably taken around 1910. On the right-hand side, with the large gateway, is the Bull Inn, whose premises backed onto the old Corn Exchange situated alongside the Cattle Market. With so much activity within a relatively small area, market days were often hectic and hazardous. Shoppers were frequently penned in doorways while flocks of sheep passed by or had to dash for cover as an escaped bull made for the proverbial china shop. It was also not uncommon for lunch-time drinkers to have their pints put in peril by a cow in search of her lost calf and on occasions the event has even made the local headlines.

27. The Bushel is sadly all that remains of this picturesque corner of the Rookery showing the inn and part of Market Place. Much of the whole area was redeveloped during the 1960s and 1970s, leaving very few of the original buildings in place. Of those that survive, the observant could pick out parts of Wellington Street and a row of weatherboarded shops in Market Street, one of which used to front an old inland smoke house. If you pay a visit to The Bushel today, you could still recognise it by its distinct style and enjoy a glass of local brew, in much the same way Charles II and his court followers are said to have done after the Restoration.

28. Simpson's has long been established in the High Street as a printer, stationer and bookseller. The shop was certainly there a century ago and the name continues to this day as Simpson and Jeffery. The premise acted as an office for the local newspaper, the Newmarket Journal and printed up a daily sheet, the Sporting News. Although the 'Journal' is still with us, published from its efficient modern office in The Rookery, the Sporting News has long since disappeared. The elaborate old shop front was right next to The Greyhound, later the Carlton, and directly opposite Goldings, another well-known Newmarket firm, established in 1864 on the site of the old palace of James I. For many years the premises was called The Palace Shop and it is said you can see remnants of the royal foundations in the shop's cellars.

29. A late morning exercise string returning to their stables along the High Street. On the right is Grafton House, known also as the King's House, and across the road is a solid brick residence, once the home of the Godolphin family. The pillared gateway on the extreme left led to another private residence, long since gone. It was demolished to give access to a new road constructed by Col. McCalmont as a more direct route between the station and the race course. Originally only a private road, the Urban Council were pleased to note in their minutes of 23rd September 1904, that they had received word from the executors of the late Col. McCalmont of their intention to dedicate 'The Avenue' to the use of the public as a highway.

The Avenue, showing Royal Entrance to Jockey Club Grounds, Newmarket

30. A northwards look down The Avenue towards the High Street, with on the right, near the man sweeping the road, the Royal Entrance to the Jockey Club grounds. On the left is one of the original, very ornate, carbon arc lamps which pioneered the new form of lighting to the town as early as 1899. Keen rivalry existed between the Gas and Electric Companies for the Public Lighting contract and in 1902 the Gas Company managed to obtain the tender for the next three years with a quote of £958. 5s. The neat rows of saplings down either side of the roadway give a clear indication of how recently The Avenue had been laid out when this picture was taken around 1909.

THE AVENUE NEWMARKET

31. A later view of The Avenue, this time looking south towards the turn-offs to Cardigan Street and Warrington Street and along the line of what was once the drive to Cheveley Park, over two miles away. Many of the impressive houses were built during the early years of this century for those involved in horseracing, whether as owners, trainers or jockeys and to this day the road continues to be one of Newmarket's prime residential areas. Although this picture was taken on a quiet spring day, it was one of the main routes to the races for punters arriving by train and on race days became a melee of horse-drawn vehicles, 'new fangled' automobiles and those using Shanks's pony.

The King's House, Newmarket.

32. The King's House occupied a prominent place in the High Street until it was demolished to make way for the King Edward VII Memorial Hall and Gardens. It stood almost opposite the Jockey Club and was originally known as Grafton House and owned by Sir Ernest Cassel until it was purchased by the King in 1904. Naturally the town was delighted that the long standing tradition of a royal residence in Newmarket was to be continued, but by March 1905 local newspapers were casting some doubt on it ever being used by His Majesty. 'Although Grafton House was reported months ago to have been purchased by the King, no sign of preparations for H.M.'s occupation is yet to be seen. He will probably continue to use his suite of apartments in the Jockey Club.'

HIGH STREET, NEWMARKET.

33. Western end of the High Street taken in the late 1920s. The very large 18th century house on the left is Godolphin House, once the home of Lord Godolphin, who imported the famous 'Godolphin' Arabian into the country in the 1700s. It is said that this horse is the ancestor of at least a third of all today's race horses and there is a memorial to him under the archway of Wandlebury House, on the outskirts of Cambridge. Attached to Godolphin House is the Masonic Club and out of sight in The Avenue, which is the turning to the left by the lamp-post, is the Scotch Tea Rooms, a favourite in the town for many years and sadly now closed down. Note the road looks in a better state of repair, no doubt due in part, to the more common use of the motor car.

34. Newmarket is tucked into a hollow at the junction of two valleys, and as this picture, taken in the 1920s, illustrates, it is easy to see why it floods from time to time, particularly after a heavy summer storm. Unfortunately, the High Street has to deal with more than one watery problem, for there are also several natural springs situated along its length. The common belief is that these give trouble every seven years and certainly, it is not uncommon for the fire engine to be seen pumping out someone's basement. One of the springs lies directly under the post office and another under Boots, the chemists. Both caused much entertainment for the locals, when, during construction work, the builders had to find a solution to one of nature's well kept secrets.

King Edward VII Memorial Hall, Newmarket

35. King Edward VII Memorial Hall was built on the site of Grafton House, as a public hall, in tribute to a monarch who had been a frequent visitor to the town during his long patronage of the Turf. In its lifetime it has been used by various groups and gatherings but none will be remembered with more humour than on 18th February 1941, the day the High Street was bombed. The post office received a direct hit, so did the White Hart and the front of the Doric Cinema, all within a few yards of the Memorial Hall where a military conference was in progress involving some five hundred officers. There were four hundred and ninety-nine very distracted men and one, quite unaffected. He was the Commanding Officer addressing the assembly, who, being totally deaf, did not even hear the explosions!

High Street and Terrace, Newmarket.

36. It was on The Terrace that children used to gather on race days to watch the carriages go past bearing 'lords and ladies' off to the course. They were also known to gather to plague the punters, who, having arrived by train in Newmarket during the morning on the racing 'Specials', had spent time quenching their thirsts before making their way, somewhat unsteadily, by foot to the Heath. In this picture, taken around the 1890s, there is a fair sprinkling of adults too, including a shop-girl leaning on the lamp-post, an obvious 'gent' striding down to the town and in the foreground, a rather regal looking perambulator of a type which was often referred to as 'the Canoe'.

37. View of The Terrace and property on the right-hand side of the High Street going towards the race course taken about 1910. From the signs over the shops we can see that the first one is Heffer's and two down belongs to Harper & Co. The decorative shop fronts must have been added at some time over the last twenty years because in the 1880s these premises were simply large houses, each with a small piece of garden running onto the pavement. They were tenanted by a saddler, a tailor and a trainer, while just along from them lived William Barrows, veterinary surgeon, and William Charles Manning, agent for the Jockey Club. His wife, Sarah, was the Club's housekeeper and in charge of preparations for any visits by royalty. Both sides of the road have cobbled drainage channels with bridged areas at regular intervals to accommodate horse-drawn vehicles turning into private entrances.

38. A long view of The Terrace end of the High Street looking back towards the Jockey Club and the shops, taken about 1912. The mature trees and graduated wall on the right hide a line of imposing houses with equally imposing names: Lushington, Clifton, Lonsdale and Richmond, Queensbury Lodge and at the very top, Glenwood Collegiate School, forerunner of the Grammar School which was later transferred to Foley House, Wellington Street. All of the houses are still in existence and recently a few have undergone extensive renovation. They certainly have great style and are perhaps those referred to in White's Directory of 1841 when it described Newmarket as being a 'handsome market town with several elegant houses and public buildings'.

39. St. Mary's lies to the north of the High Street and formed the focal point for Newmarket's early development within the parish of Exning. Mediaeval in origin, initially it was chapel-of-ease to St. Martin's, before becoming a parish church in its own right in the 16th century. It was however, heavily restored at one time and the Chancel was almost entirely rebuilt in 1856. Like most churches in the past, St. Mary's played its part in the welfare and education of the community, with a St. Mary's Board School under its jurisdiction and several charities to administer, including one for 'Bread and Beef' which continues to be doled out to this day but now in the form of cash.

St. Mary's Church, Newmarket.

40. An Edwardian equivalent of a modern aerial photograph, known as a Bird's Eye View and in this instance, taken from the top of St. Mary's parish church, looking across the Square to the famous covered ride in the middle distance. The birthday cake-like building on the opposite side of the green is the Wesleyan Chapel built in 1841, and next door, fulfilling man's spiritual and temporal needs within the space of a few yards, stands the Five Bells! Since this view was taken, much of the green has vanished to make way for a road. The Chapel and the Five Bells still remain, as do the elegant properties adjoining and those on the right, but the more humble cottages to the left, together with all those that once made up Ice Well Hill, Victory Lane and Ward's Alley, have been demolished and replaced by high-rise flats.

41. A rare glimpse of Drapery Row in the days before demolition men reduced it to an open space with just The Bushel, on the right, left as a landmark. Originally it linked Market Street to Wellington Street and was one of several lanes and alleyways making up the old Rookery area, a hive of small residential and commercial properties. It was also an area with more than its fair share of inns and brewhouses and often these were sited only a few yards away from each other, as in this picture. Opposite The Bushel stands the Woolpack, and both were popular drinking venues for the visiting race-gangs from the big cities. It was customery for various towns to adopt certain inns and rivalry was keen, often resulting in 'breaches of the peace'. In the past The Bushel has been able to claim monarchy among its customers, as it is said Charles II enjoyed watching cock-fighting mains in the inn's cellars.

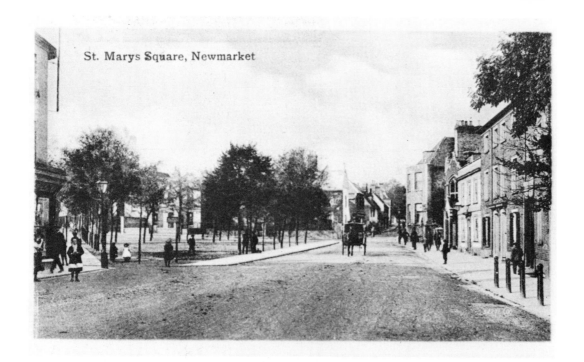

St. Marys Square, Newmarket

42. St. Mary's Square and Mill Hill around the time of the First World War. Much of the right-hand side of the postcard would be recognisable today, beginning with the houses adjoining Foley House, then up past the Five Bells to the Methodist Chapel. The property on the left is still a shop but most of the grass and trees have vanished. All the houses in the distance on Ice Well Hill were demolished about twenty years ago, but before that they formed a very close-knit community, particularly so during the late eighteen hundreds. The dwellings were humble, often overcrowded and housed some of the town's poorer people. When typhoid broke out in 1891 it claimed several victims and the cause was eventually traced to the Hill's wells which had become infected with raw sewage.

ALL SAINTS CHURCH, NEWMARKET.

43. Although of humble status, being simply a chapel-of-ease to St. Mary's, Woodditton until it became a church in its own right in 1868, All Saints was adopted as the Court Chapel and several members of the Palace staff have memorials in the church, including Tregonwell Frampton, trainer for a succession of monarchs until his death in 1727. Sadly, by 1874 the fabric of the building was in such a terrible state, with windows nailed in and even the supporting pillars giving serious concern, that it was decided to completely rebuild and in doing so, make better use of the site by literally 'turning the church round'. This, being something of an anomaly, visitors who study an old print of the church in the early 19th century, are often at a lose to say why things don't look quite the same!

44. Palace House Stables taken at the turn of the century — and not a wisp of straw showing. In the background the top of All Saints tower reminds us both royal residences were built in the Cambridgeshire half of Newmarket and that the Court once worshipped under the church's roof. The first palace, built by James I around 1609, occupied a site on the High Street slightly lower down than the royal residence built by Charles II after the Restoration. It is Charles' palace, once described by one of his contemporaries as 'a mean enough dwelling' that probably bequeathed the name and possibly some of the brickwork to Palace House Stables.

45. The Three Tuns, one of Newmarket's now long forgotten public houses, photographed about 1891. It used to stand on the left-hand side of Market Place, a small recess off Market Street, and practically opposite the entrance to Drapery Row. For many years it was kept by the Double family who originated from Cavendish in Suffolk. The Census lists widow Sophy as being head of the family, with son Charles as the official innkeeper and younger children George and Sarah also helping out behind the bar. At some stage around 1880 the small adjoining cottage was taken over as an off-licence selling wines, as the notice in the window indicates, but the whole scene changed at the beginning of this century when the Three Tuns ceased to exist.

DUCHESS DRIVE NEWMARKET

46. Duchess Drive, looking very different from today, was named after Elizabeth, Duchess of Rutland, who together with her husband, John Henry, fifth Duke of Rutland, resided at Cheveley Hall in the early 1800s. The couple had wed soon after his coming-of-age and it is said that they shared a life of uninterrupted happiness until her death in 1825. During her life time she undertook much redesigning of the Rutland seat, Belvoir Castle, of the surrounding countryside and of the grounds of Cheveley Hall, but she is best known for the long treelined drive leading from the town to their house. After her death, the Duke continued to entertain 'many ladies and gentlemen of mark and fashion' including Beau Brummel, and when Cheveley Hall became too delapidated, the Palace was put at his disposal.

47. A view of the Rous Memorial Hospital, Upper Station Road (now known as Old Station Road), taken soon after its completion. It was originally built in 1879 in memory of Admiral Rous, a great patron of the Turf, on land given by Sir Richard Wallace, and the general plan was of a pavillon, having beds for ten people. Patients were mainly admitted from the racing fraternity, although on occasions others were given treatment in an emergency, like the young man who fell from the scaffolding during the construction of the post office in 1885. The hospital continued in use until 1966 when it was purchased by the Council and converted into homes for the elderly. During the conversion a tablet was discovered which said that it had been placed there by H.R.H. Prince of Wales in 1887, to commemorate a gift made by the inhabitants of Newmarket for the extension of the Hospital, so that female patients could be admitted in celebration of Queen Victoria's Jubilee.

48. A later view of the Rous Memorial Hospital of Upper Station Road, taken sometime during the summer of 1905. The photograph clearly illustrates the poor state of the town's roads at the time and gives us a fair idea why there were so many complaints. This particular stretch proved additionally hazardous as it had to cope with race day traffic as well before the opening of The Avenue. Many rye comments were passed about it being a 'jolly good thing there was a hospital handy'. In the distance is the Clock Tower, Newmarket's ever present monument, and in the foreground, one of the highly ornamental gas lamps, which at the turn of the century, used New Welsbach Incandescent bulbs giving between 75 - 80 candle power each.

49. It seems little in Newmarket strays far from some connection with the horse. Even this pretty photograph taken in the spring of 1905 in Old Station Road, then known as Upper Station Road, tells us by the sign that it is the entrance to G. Barrows, veterinary surgeon. George Barrows was in fact, a member of a highly respected family in the town, several of which were involved in one or other forms of medicine. Of vets in particular, there was often scepticism, as many of the racing fraternity preferred to prepare their own remedies for equine complaints. However, towards the end of the 1800s a certain recognition was creeping in to the profession as the Racing Illustrated commented in its hallowed pages: 'Members of the veterinary profession are nowadays, as a rule, highly intelligent and pleasant gentlemen, often possessed of a rich fund of anecdotes.' Praise indeed!

No. 3412

Parr & Son's Copyright Series.

50. This view down Exeter Road, past The Watercourse, Waterwitch House and out towards Tan Gallop, clearly illustrates Newmarket's expansion during the 19th century. Neat dwellings built on the principle of two up, two down, each with a small front garden to prevent people looking in through the parlour window as they pass. The woman and child on the left are standing on the corner of Baker's Row, a group of cottages constructed of rough flint, a popular local building material, and similarly the premises on the opposite side, known as The Mount, is built in the same way. Apart from the addition of television aerials which have sprung up on the high chimney stacks, the road has remained virtually unchanged to this day, and those frozen in time by the camera's lens seventy years ago would have little trouble recognising their whereabouts.

51. A typical race day scene on the Rowley Mile which may well have given rise to a statement issued in October 1880: 'The Jockey Club is to organise special staff to clear racecourses of bad characters. The detectives will be picked from various large towns, as most of the notorious offenders will be known to them. It may be said, that the rowdyism and violence of the lower strata reflects the general condition of the Turf, as owners of horses regard winning as the great object to be obtained.' It would seem the detectives were not all that successful, as there are continual references over the next few years to the 'state of the Turf', the increase in bad language and plague of pick-pocketing.

52. Fred Archer is regarded as the greatest jockey who ever lived, for although his life was short, his dedication to racing was beyond question. He was eighteen years old when he rode as first jockey for Matt Dawson of Heath House. Six years later he was made a partner and fell in love with Matt's niece Helen. They married in January 1883 and lived in domestic bliss at Falmouth House until their son was born the following January and died within a few hours of birth. Helen took months to recover but was eventually delivered of a daughter in the autumn of 1885. Unfortunately, she herself died the next day and Fred Archer gave in to black depression. Despite a trip to America, little could be done to ease his gloom and 1886 was to prove his last season. He shot himself after the final meeting at Lewes and was buried with those he loved, in Newmarket's cemetery.

53. Portland House, typical of the substantial residences built in and around the town for patrons of the Turf and their trainers. Most were constructed during the hey-day of Victorian expansion; a few, elegantly Georgian, but in general, what they lacked in style they made up for in solidness. They were usually set amidst their own extensive grounds, where, with plenty of labour on hand, it was possible to indulge in the latest craze for importing all manner of foreign trees and plants. As you wander through the town today, it is fascinating to wonder about these fine houses previous owners and to imagine what tales the bricks could tell, if only they could talk!

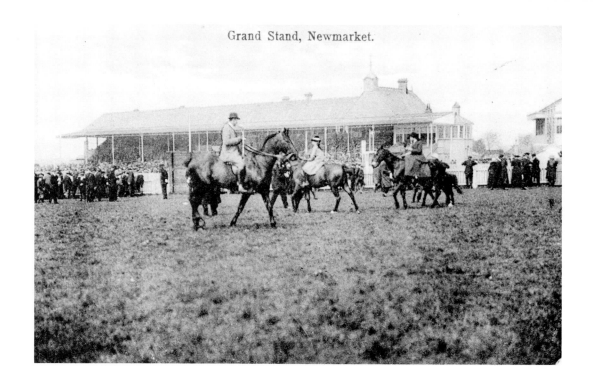

Grand Stand, Newmarket.

54. Grand Stand, Newmarket, around the time of the First World War. It was quite natural for race-goers to spill out onto the course between races and to ride over the turf, as shown here. Note too, that the ladies are riding side-saddle. When this picture was taken, the stand had been in existence for almost forty years, but comments from 1874 tell us that 'the racecourse lacks one of the many accessories to be found on every other course in the land'. It was also said to have 'only a miserable weighing room and no proper dressing-room for the jockeys'. Members of the Jockey Club were housed in little better than a shed (perhaps that's why one got built soon after). As for the general public, they had to stay on horseback or in their broughams for comfort and safety.

Newmarket   Ditch Side Stand and July Course

55. A view across the July Course towards the Members Stand, on the right, and the Silver Ring or Half-Crown Enclosure, on the left, taken about 1898. These stands have now vanished, although the public can still view the racing from this side of the course, either by the rails or from Devil's Dyke beyond. It is interesting to note some of the problems of photography at the turn of the century. One 'Artiste' covering the Course for the Princess of Wales Stakes used 'fourteen plates in a vain endeavour to get a single reproduction'. He put his misfortune down to the black skies and heavy background of trees and was mightily relieved when the sun finally came out and he managed a few shots of the races later in the meet.

56. Devil's Ditch or Devil's Dyke as it is more commonly known, is a huge earthworks thrown up as an ancient line of defence across the Cambridgeshire/Suffolk countryside. No one is totally sure who built it, but popular belief credits the Iceni in their struggle to survive the attacks of other tribes, and later, the Romans. Whoever it was, they had a mammoth task, for the bank of chalky soil stands as high as sixty feet in places and stretches eight miles, beginning in the edge of fen village of Reach and ending in the woods of Woodditton. Rumour has it that the old custom of carrying a coffin along the path, to maintain it as a public right of way, was adhered to well into this century but I don't think that right has ever been in dispute. Just like the young man in the photograph the public can still enjoy the pleasures of the Dyke and on race days it provides a magnificent free view of the races.

Moulton Paddocks. Newmarket. Residence of Sir Ernest Cassell. № 75.

57. Moulton Paddocks, a typical flint and brick Victorian mansion, a mile outside of Newmarket towards Bury St. Edmunds, and once the residence of Sir Ernest Cassel, a great patron of the Turf circa 1900. Sir Ernest was quite a character and credited with what is commonly known as 'The Horse Story'. It appears Sir Ernest asked the advice of Lord Marcus Beresford over what he should have painted on the sides of his horse-boxes. 'Should it be Sir Ernest Cassel or Sir Ernest Cassel, KCMG.' 'Oh,' replied Lord Marcus, 'if I were you, I should put Sir Ernest Cassel, KCM on the outside and the 'G' inside.'

Newmarket   Old Cambridgeshire Stand and Course

The Wrench Series No. 6765

58. Anyone studying the history and lay-out of Newmarket's racecourses could be forgiven for getting confused by the sheer number and the times they have been altered. This picture shows the Old Cambridgeshire Stand and Course which at one time carried on in a slight left turn from the Beacon Course, to end at the Top of the Town, or as we know it, opposite the cemetery. Such were the problems, that on Cambridgeshire Day, most of the racing was viewed from the shorter course, but then, having watched the horses in the paddock and going down to the start, spectators had to trudge a fair way across the open Heath to watch them go past the winning post. Fortunately things have changed today!

59. A corner of the 'Birdcage' on the old Cambridgeshire course taken about 1896, showing the racing elite waiting for the numbers to go up on the board. Despite there being very few lady owners at the time and no lady jockeys or trainers, the race course was still considered a place to be seen for the 'fashionable' females of the day. This photograph was captured at the last meeting of the season and obviously a day for a top coat and fur trim. Even so, the ladies have really gone to town on their hats! The name Birdcage was perpetuated in the town's Birdcage Walk and some of Newmarket's older residents can remember the area before it was altered into the busy junction that stands there today.

60. John Dawson, pictured in 1896, one of the four famous Dawson brothers who were all involved in racing during the second half of the 1800s. Three of them, Mat, Joe and John, had establishments at Newmarket, John's being at Warren House, where he trained for Prince Batthyany, a Hungarian nobleman and owner of Galopin, the 1875 Derby winner. John's daughter married his brother Mat's jockey and partner at Heath House, Fred Archer, thus keeping things very much in the family, but tragically, both she and Archer were dead by 1886. On his retirement from racing in 1900, John handed over Warren House to his son, George.

61. Newmarket and flat racing are synonymous and it is hard to imagine that steeplechasing once occupied a place in the racing calendar too. The course was known as the Link Farm Course and was situated on land owned by Col. McCalmont, whose brainchild it was. Facilities were said to be excellent, with a properly constructed stand as protection from the keen east wind which blew straight across the open land from the direction of the Fens. It seems likely that despite Col. McCalmont's interest, the idea was short-lived, as although mention of steeplechasing is made in the 1880s and 1890s, nothing of significance is mentioned afterwards and the course is not marked at all on the 1926 map of the district. Whether the weather was a deciding factor or lack of interest, we do not know, but newspapers of the day are always reporting that meetings have had to be abandoned or post-posted because of adverse conditions.

62. Before the stand was built on the Rowley Mile it was said that there was only a 'miserable weighing room and no proper dressing room' for the jockeys. If that was thought primitive, I wonder what the writer would have said about this photograph, taken in a stable yard about 1896 – not so much a question of measuring accurately, more a case of as near as possible. As for the dressing room, well, what better than behind the straw in the background! Apprentice jockeys began riding very young, sometimes even before reaching their teens. Consequently there was a large turn-over in apprentices as they often out grew the job between the ages of thirteen and eighteen.

63. Race-goers came in all shapes and forms and from all walks of life, especially after the introduction of the 'race day specials' by the railway company. By the late 1920s however, char-à-bancs were also a regular feature of any race meeting. Trips were organised by enterprising local bus companies and it became the 'done things' for daring young men to get toffed up in their best suits, don a carnation and cut a dash on the Rowley Mile. This shot was taken on route and even the driver's entered into the spirit of things by tagging on the end. Looking at their smiling faces over half a century later, one can't help wondering whether they were still smiling on the way home or whether they had lost all their money on a 'dead cert'.

64. It was the rolling heathland surrounding Newmarket that first attracted James I to hunt and hawk there in 1605. The intervening centuries have simply provided time to turn a natural advantage into a vast expanse of carefully cultivated green, expertly managed and groomed by groundsmen in the employ of the Jockey Club. When this photograph was taken in the 1890s it must have been an awesome task to maintain the huge acreage in prime condition and a never ending job for these two horses engaged in rolling the 'Long Hill'. Sometimes it got so hot for them, exposed on the heath, that they had to wear bonnets to ward off sunstroke. Today, those same acres are kept in trim by one of the widest mowing machines in the world, but it is still a never ending task!

65. A strong portrait of the Duchess of Montrose, one of racing's famous patroness's. She was reputed to be a redhead with a temper to match and many stories abound of her way with servants. Her second husband, Stirling Crawfurd, also a great lover of racing, died in Cannes in 1883, but the Duchess was determined his body should be brought back to rest in Newmarket. She set about having a mausoleum built next to her own chapel of St. Agnes in the Bury Road and when it was finished in 1885, had the coffin transported home. It arrived by train late one November night and was taken across the Heath to be interred at midnight, the service attended by only the priest, the Duchess and a close friend.

66. Newmarket has been served by three railway stations at different times. The first, pictured above, was an impressive Baroque affair built in 1848 when the railway opened. In 1885, Warren Hill Station came into use for the specific purpose of relieving some of the extra traffic on race-days, but this became virtually obsolete when, in 1902, a fine, new station was constructed slightly to the south of the old one. For a while, the original grand structure was used as a handling base for the transportation of racehorses, however, despite strong protests, it was finally demolished in 1981 after years of neglect. Its epitaph was perhaps best conveyed by a comment from Pevsner, 'if it is allowed to disappear, England will have lost one of its most spectacular railway stations'. Many people would agree with him.

67. Warren Hill tunnel was a feat of mid-19th century engineering that enabled the Newmarket to Ipswich line to pass under the chalk of Warren Hill and the Bury Road, to emerge on the other side, to the right of Bedford Lodge. This was just one of the many innovations undertaken as the rail system advanced through East Anglia, but tunnels were not without their moments of excitement as a newspaper report of 1883 tells us. 'Passengers experienced considerable discomfort while passing through the Warren Hill tunnel on Tuesday. It appears that the wheels of the engine did not 'bite' the metals and the fireman, getting down to remedy this, missed the train in the smoke and steam with which the tunnel was filled. The driver went backwards and forwards for a minute or two in an effort to find him but failing to do this, he proceeded to the Bury end of the tunnel. Meanwhile the fireman had made his way out of the tunnel at the Newmarket end and running across the heath, rejoined the train at the other side.' That's what I call devotion to duty!

68. Boxing a horse, particularly a highly strung thoroughbred, can be a difficult business at the best of times as any stableman will confirm but when this photograph was taken in the 1890s, it was also a novelty. Transporting horses about the country by train brought a new element to the racing scene, fast travel. It was no longer necessary to make elaborate plans for getting horses to courses well in advance, so they could be rested before their race day, rail travel in specially constructed coaches ment there and back in a day sometimes. Newmarket's three different stations have all acted as loading platforms in their time, but when this shot was captured, the original, 1848 Baroque building was still in general use.

69. A later photograph of the difficult business of loading valuable livestock. Just like today, straw was laid down to encourage horses to be sure-footed and often they were also blind-folded, like some are when they enter modern starting gates. This long shot shows off the attractive old gas lamps that used to light the station built in 1902. When it was demolished in the 1960s, during British Rails efforts to streamline the eastern region, the lamps, together with the elaborate ironwork which used to hold up the platform roof, were destroyed, and with the exception of odd pieces that ended up as collector's items, were buried under tons of rubble.

EAST CAMBS.
(NEWMARKET) ELECTION,
—1910—

Photo: Bolton, Ely.

SIR CHARLES D. ROSE

THE LIBERAL & FREE TRADE
CANDIDATE.

70. Politics have always been the second subject of conversation in Newmarket and especially so before the First World War when both the Liberals and the Conservatives regularly held 'successful' Smoking Concerts in support of their causes. In 1910, Sir Charles D. Rose, the Liberal and Free Trade candidate, of Suffolk House, Newmarket, found himself campaigning for the fourth time, although as he freely admitted in his election address, after seven years in Parliament, he might well have stood down if the national situation had not been so desperate. He was referring to the unprecedented action of the House of Lords in refusing to pass into Law the financial provisions for the annual expenditure and no doubt this, together with his comment that 'he would support a measure for the Parliamentary Enfranchisement of Women' gave the 'gentlemen' something to talk about at those 'Smoking Concerts'.

NEWMARKET CAMP 1914

71. Not for the first time in the 'Great War' was the Heath used as a camping ground for the army. Three centuries earlier, during the English Civil War, Cromwell's troops had been encamped in much the same place and later, having held Charles I under house arrest within his own royal palace, they escorted him to eventual death and left his Newmarket residence in virtual ruin. This picture clearly shows us that having the military on their doorstep was a novelty for the local people and biking or strolling out to have a look at all the activity, proved a fascinating diversion from the grim news coming out of France throughout the summer of 1914.

72. A wedding scene like many others from all over the country as soldiers came home on leave and wed their sweethearts before going off to the trenches in the First World War. In this photograph, taken in 1916, some of Newmarket's well-known surnames were being linked; the Bishop's, the Fuller's, Challis's and Parr's. Most lived in the parish of St. Mary's, either in Lowther Street or on nearby Ice Well Hill, where in peacetime the menfolk worked for the local council or in the stables. Sadly few of the young men doing their best to impress the camera, ever survived the effects of the war but the names are still going strong today.

73. Sending troops off to war with rousing military music and the best wishes of civilians ringing in their ears, became the established pattern of such events as Britain quickly realised it wasn't going to be 'all over by Christmas'. For the 1st Battalion Herefords, seen here marching down the High Street in 1915, it must have seemed they were leaving the haven of a peaceful market town, for the closest thing to hell on earth. Yet, within a year, Newmarket's peace was to be breeched, as Zeppelin raids over East Anglia became ever more common and the town itself was bombed during April 1916, killing 'a man and a horse'.

74. Newmarket's Fire Brigade pictured in 1885 posing with their new fire engine outside their headquarters in Albion Street. They were much sought after in more ways than one, for, not only were they in the front-line for putting out fires but they were also much in demand for church parades, cutting a colourful dash in their uniforms decorated with braid and brass buttons. On several occasions they formed part of the Lord Mayor's Show and one can only imagine the pride they must have felt at the honour. Just like today though, it seems November 5th brought its own particular problems. Brief entries in local newspapers often relate to fires caused by the celebration of the 'Gunpowder Plot'. Then, as now, straw stacks and thatched roofs were most at risk.

75. A unique photograph taken by a local photographer — the day the balloon went up! Originally it was thought to have been taken about 1914, but it seems more likely to have an earlier date because the photographer, H.R. Sherborn, who had a studio in the High Street, was dead by 1901. Hundreds flocked to watch the occasion, donning their best clothes and fanciest hats to make a real day of it and completely encircling an area known as the 'Birdcage' in their attempts to get a closer look. In the background is the flint wall of the town cemetery and the horses and carts are drawn up on the road to Cambridge. The rolling countryside beyond is the parish of Woodditton.

76. A lovely study of a Newmarket young lady taken just before the turn of the century, but it is not so much the subject that provides the interest, as the photographer. Henry Robert Sherborn lived in Wellington Street with his wife and children but was shrewd enough to set up his business in a prominent position in the High Street, right next to the Rutland Arms. Early mounted prints of his declare he is simply F.R.P.S. but by the time this photograph was taken, he had the Prince of Wales feathers up and could obviously claim royal fame. Sadly his vast collection of photographs and negatives do not seem to have survived intact, although those that are still around firmly establish him as a talent of note, both of people and events.